Mag & Secrets *Of* *Step* Parenting

DOs and DON'Ts For Building Love Together
Even In a Blended Family

MORIN GRAY, PhD

MORIN GRAY, PhD

Copyright©2021 Morin Gray, PhD

All Rights Reserved

INTRODUCTION 4

THE BEGINNING 4

CHAPTER ONE 7

THE STEP-PARENT 7
WHO IS A GOOD STEP-PARENT? 8
DAILY CHALLENGES OF STEPPARENTS 11

CHAPTER TWO 15

GOOD STEP-CHILD/STEP-PARENT'S RELATIONSHIPS 15
WHY IS IT IMPORTANT? 15
STEP-PARENTING STYLE FOR POSITIVE PARENTING 18
TIPS FOR BUILDING A GOOD STEP-CHILD/STEP-PARENT RELATIONSHIP 18

CHAPTER THREE 25

EFFECTIVE STEP-PARENTING 25
THE DOS 25
THE DON'TS (DO NOTS) 33

CHAPTER FOUR 37

BAD STEP-PARENTING 37
CAUSES OF BAD STEP-PARENTING 37

CHAPTER FIVE 45

EFFECTS OF POOR STEP-PARENTING, AND SOLUTIONS 45

| Solutions to Bad Step-Parenting | 49 |

CHAPTER SIX   53

Conclusion   53

MORIN GRAY, PhD

INTRODUCTION

The Beginning

Parenting is unarguably one of life's most rewarding endeavors. It would give you joy and most times it might sour your mood. It can be exhilarating and yet still be overwhelming and challenging. All the same, it is absolutely a unique feeling everyone should get.

Becoming a step-parent, which can happen because you are marrying someone who already has kids can be exciting, scary, and overwhelming, all at once. The feeling might differ with different people.

If you have kids, you'll be blending families and having to make them establish the bond that siblings have. If you do not, you'll get to live with a younger person and have to help build and shape his or her life and character as a parent.

There are cases where new families or individuals get to blend and get along smoothly without problems. But then, sometimes there are challenges.

There is no best way to be a great step-parent, no magic formula, no secret recipe, nothing. Figuring everything out, aside from your day-to-day responsibilities may also lead to confusion. But then, all successful step-parents share a thing or two in common, which we'll talk about.

Good parenting is no child's play. A great deal of consistency, routine, and other factors are necessary to give your child (Yes, the child is now your child) the required sense of comfort, attention, discipline, and all-rounded training, because that's what good parenting is all about; bringing up a good child.

CHAPTER ONE

The Step-Parent

Once you have a baby, you automatically become a parent. You become a father or a mother at once. You get to do things like cuddling a child at night when he or she is crying, washing and changing diapers, breastfeeding and all that comes with the territory.

You become a step-parent if you get married to someone who already has a kid or children. At the onset, you might feel like an outsider. There are years of shared memories, and experiences between the members of the biological family that a step-parent will never be a part of.

But then, with time, the whole family would grow into something new, great, and wonderful. You'll do fine.

Who Is A Good Step-Parent?

This is more complex than just being a parent. A good step-parent has to do so much more. You are building a new connection and a new relationship and the outcome will affect your life, the child's life, and the family.

A good step-parent builds this new connection, develops this new relationship, and generally affects the life of the stepchild positively.

Here are some attributes to check for in a good step-parent:

- A good step-parent loves unconditionally.
- A good step-parent understands the stepchild and goes out of his or her way to try to understand the child's behavior, wants, and desires.
- A good step-parent is involved in a child's life.

- A good step-parent trains the stepchild to learn necessary morals, character, and beliefs.
- A good step-parent is committed to making the stepchild better.
- .A good step-parent supports the stepchild's growth.

There is so much to be a good stepdad or stepmom. Firstly, good parenting should involve both parents. It is therefore important that both parents (the biological and step-parents) work together to provide the child with the sense of having a full family, even if one of the parents might not be his or her real parent.

Being a good step-parent is a decision that stems from wanting something better for yourself, your partner, and your stepchild or children and putting the extra effort to make sure it works. The overall effect would be a more peaceful and loving family.

The concept of achieving the badge of a good step-parent is not a destination but a continuing journey for all mothers and fathers and like every journey, there are bound to be challenges that would make you fail. It is necessary to note these challenges and learn from them to be able to avoid these mistakes that so many would-have-been 'good parents' had made.

With the increasing requirements and demands of parenthood, many parents are having a hard time holding their talk more of a step-parent. A stepparent is being faced with more challenges than ever faced in the history of parenting. A new environment, a new child, and perhaps the hovering presence of an ex, to mention a few.

Maintaining a proper balance between your new parenting role if you had never been a parent yet and working would also prove to become more hectic as the workplace is becoming more demanding, despite the rise of technology. As a result, step-parent are becoming overwhelmed and parenting suffers.

Daily Challenges of Stepparents

Here are some of the challenges stepparents have to face in their daily lives that are making the task of parenting seem hard:

Scarcity of Time

One of the most important parenting challenges that stepparents face these days is the unavailability of quality time to spend with their children and stepchildren.

Most stepparents struggle daily with a plethora of duties and obligations that they have to meet up with or deliver. Completing daily office operations, taking care of some or even most of the house chores, especially if the kids are way younger, looking after the children, and after all these, trying to sneak in time for your partner.

With all of these, it becomes impossible for the average step-parent to have enough valuable time to talk, play or build the necessary connections necessary with the children.

In this kind of situation, children would soon start having the feeling of being neglected and unloved, which might not be true, and start seeking the presence of their 'other parent', which might bring problems into the family.

Negative reactions from your stepchild's other parent.
The stepchild's other parent might prove to be burdensome and bring up trouble. Especially if he or she does not like the new step-parent or feel that the new parent is the cause of the split.

Your stepchild's other parent might continually say negative comments or haul criticism at your good effort and these might be a challenge and might affect the relationship with your spouse and your family generally.

Different Approach To Parenting

It is a fact that different people have different preferred styles of parenting. If both parents have different approaches to parenting and cannot come together to accept or make a compromise in picking one and affecting it properly, this would be a challenge and might lead to problems in the family

The difference can be in their style of discipline or mode of showing affection, however little or big it is, there will be disagreement except both partners learn to handle it properly.

Difficulty in Bonding

Another major challenge that step-parents often face is the inability or difficulty to create emotional bonding with the stepchild.

This is most difficult with older children who might have already bonded with their biological parents and do not see the need for another parent.

Younger children might be easier to bond and connect with. But then, there is always a difficulty in trying to get this emotional connection and it might pose a challenge and become a problem if it takes too long to happen.

Bonds are built when parents spend considerable time having fun, sharing secrets, learning, or teaching their children. If your stepchild or children do not agree to open up, there are chances that it would be difficult to create a child-parent relationship.

Children end up living with their parents as aliens, they might not be able to open up or talk about things. As a result, they might resort to their peers for this bonding and most times peer pressure might not be the right kind

CHAPTER TWO

Good Step-Child/Step-Parent's Relationships

Why Is It Important?

Being a good step-parent is fulfilling on its own, the icing would be if and when you grow a productive relationship with your child. You become an anchor and would be filling up space in your child's life.

Modern family relationships can be burdensome at times, with so many activities that need to be done and the accompanying stress, it becomes difficult in a way to build good and awesome relationships.

Good step-parents want the best for their children, and building a good step-child/step-parent relationship can help lead to better lives for the children and happy home for the family.

The good step-child/step-parent relationship helps foster the physical, emotional, and social development of the child and is a unique kind of bond that every child and parent would value and enjoy if developed.

This step-child/step-parent relationship, either good or bad lays the foundation for a child's personality build-up, lifestyle, life choice, and general outlook of life.

A bad step-child/step-parent relationship affects the child's social, physical, and mental health negatively. It creates a gap between a parent and child, affects communication, and can lead to problems in the future.

A good step-child/step-parent would include the following essentials and benefit listed below:
Children who grow with a secure, robust, and healthy attachment to their parents tend to have a

better understanding of meaningful relationships and would grow up having happy and content relationships with others in their life.

Young adults who grew up having a good relationship are better at managing stress and difficult situations.

A good step-child/step-parent relationship helps in the development of a child's mental, emotional, and linguistic growth and helps them feel secure.

A child that grows to have a healthy relationship with his or her parents/ step- parents tend to exhibit optimistic and confident social behavioral traits and would have a better outlook on life.

Excellent social and academic skills are developed by healthy parents' involvement and intervention in the child's day-to-day life.

A secure attachment would lead to healthy cognitive and social skills.

Step-children will also gain problem-solving skills that are necessary to help them navigate through life and they'll also come to love you.

Step-Parenting Style for Positive Parenting

The concepts of step-parenting do not have a 'one size fit all method. Stepparents have to change and adapt as the children grow and the need to do so arises.

Tips for Building a Good Step-Child/Step-Parent Relationship

Here are some tips that would help your positive parenting scheme and help you in building a good step-child/step-parent relationship:

Warm, Loving, and Caring Interactions
Stepparents who converse with their children warmly and lovingly tend to help their children become better with communication and would eliminate fear and tension from the relationship.

Every stepparent should see the chances of interacting with their children as an opportunity to build a connection, to teach, and become friends with them. Try to give off warm expressions, eye contact, smiles, and encouragement as all these would help positively develop the child.

Boundaries, Rules, and Regulations
As much as you should be a warm and loving step-parent. It is important to set up boundaries and rules to guide your child in all they do.

Stepchildren tend to want to be rebellious, especially the older ones and want to explore everything. It is necessary to put up structures for their guidance and good.

Setting rules should not be inhibiting. You should talk to your stepchildren about what you expect of them and make them understand the reasons behind every rule.

Listening and empathize with your stepchild:

Most Step - parents always want to talk and give instruction all the time. Most times it is better to listen. By listening to your stepchildren you get to learn a lot of things that would help you become a better step-parent.

It is of great importance to be sensitive to your child's feelings. These little ones are humans too and have feelings and emotions. Make them know that you understand what they might be going through, especially the ones in their teenage age. Reassure them that you are there to help them whenever they have any problem.

Problem Solving
As the child grows up, he or she will be faced with life's challenges and problems that will need to be solved. You must teach your stepchild about problem-solving.

Teach them to always brace up to situations and give them real-life situations to find solutions to things, to deal with difficulties in the appropriate ways.

Solving problems by yourself is another way to teach them this. Since parents are the ultimate model for their children.

Strengthen the Step - Child/Step - Parent Relationship

Forming the best type of stepchild/stepparent relationship involves building connections and bonds. Here are some tips necessary to help you strengthen bonds and develop connections with your child and generally build up your child-parent relationship

Tell and Show Your Step-Children That You Love Them

It is normal for parents to love their children, but then you must tell your stepchild that you love them and do things that make them know that you mean what you say. Simple words like 'I love you can mean a lot.

Even when you must discipline your stepchild, you should be able to send across the message they are receiving punishments, not because you do not love them, but because you did not like the behavior they exhibited.

Play Together
Playing with your step-children is very important for their development and can help both of you develop some important life skills. Also, the fun and fond memories would help build the connection necessary in a step-child/step-parent relationship.

Be Available
You must make out sufficient time to be with your step-children without any distraction. They may miss their biological parents and would need companionship. Spending a ten-minute-a-day daily uninterrupted time session with your step-child can work a great deal in making your step-child/step-parent relationship better.

MORIN GRAY, PhD

Eat Meals Together

Eating together as a family is a very vital part of family bonding. It sets the stages for family conversations and discussions, which are important to help the child's communication with you.

Make out time for each Child

Whether it is your biological child or your step-child. It is very important to try to reach out to each one individually.

Personal quality time with a parent works better in building deeper connections than spending time with the children all at once.

This doesn't in any way undermine the importance of spending quality time together as a family.

CHAPTER THREE

Effective Step-Parenting

Raising kids could be tough, whether they are your biological children or stepchildren. Notwithstanding, if done right, would yield results that every parent and step-parent would be proud of. Thus it is necessary to do it right.

Here are some tips to help you make effective step-parenting possible:

The Dos

Boosting Your Child's Self Esteem
A child starts developing the consciousness of being, the feeling of self very early in life.

They see themselves through the eyes of the closest adult, your voice tone, your body expression, and language are absorbed to become a part of the personality they would become.

Your reaction also plays a vital role in determining and building up your step-child's self-esteem too.

It is therefore important that step-parents look for ways to affect their step-children in the most positive way. Praising their every accomplishment, however, small would make them feel better and proud. Letting them do things independently would make them believe more in themselves.

In contrast to belittling comments or ill-favored comparison. Stepparents should avoid making ill statements or saying bad words as ways to get back at their stepchildren for wrongdoing. It is important to try not to damage your step-child psychologically. Instead, make them feel better and boost their self-esteem.

Notice Them Doing Well

Stepparents fall into the trap of repeatedly scolding and reacting negatively to the step-child's wrongdoings. A child would mostly do wrong. But then, the negative reaction that parents always give off makes things worse than better.

People tend to shrink or become worse with constant negative reactions and would become better if they received more positive feedback and encouragement or support, even children.

The trick here is to try to notice more of what your step-child is doing right and compliment them or encourage them. You could even buy them gifts for doing well. This way, they always want to do better and gradually would stay away from whatever wrongdoings you had been noticing.

Set limits and principles and be consistent with your discipline

The aim of disciplining your stepchild is to help them learn and choose acceptable behavior and imbibe better traits. Discipline is important for growth and development.

Establishing house rules help the stepchild to understand what is expected of him and develop self-control. These rules are different for each household and family and there are prescribed punishments for flaunting those rules. Parents must be consistent with the consequences or punishment set to be meted out.

Do not set rules and not help them keep to it. Do not prescribe punishment and let it slide. It gives them the chance to do more, after all, you might let it slide. Being consistent helps you teach your step-children and make them do the good things that are expected of them.

Be a Good Role Model
Children learn a lot from what their parents do than what they say. Before you blow off the top or

lash out angrily. It is important to be conscious of who is watching.

Do what you expect them to emulate, do not do one thing, and expect them to do another. You are the role model your stepchild has now and you must be a good role model. Give compliments, show gratitude, help others and treat people the way you expect people to treat you, even your kids.

Make Communication a Priority
Do not be an authoritarian. You must allow for communication between yourself and your stepchildren.

Give explanations for your decisions and seek the same from them. Make them understand that their opinions matter, and it is valuable in the family.

Children get to learn to be open-minded and non-judgmental in this way. They learn to be expressive and problem solvers and even team players. Since they take part in making decisions, it becomes easier for them to carry out tasks without being coerced.

Be Flexible and Willing To Adjust Your Step - Parenting Style

The challenges you face in making your step-child/step-parent relationship better maybe because you have very unrealistic expectations of your step-child. Thinking in a way that defines 'my step-child should be this or that by now is more damaging than encouraging.

You must find out where the problem lies and be willing to change and make things better.

A change in environment can help reduce the tendency of saying 'no' to your step-child and equally reduce the frustration that comes along with it.

A change in attitude can help increase the bond between you and your child and make him or her feel secure and be able to make better conversations

As your children grow also, you'll have to adapt your parenting style to match their age. A stepchild in his or her teenage age would not be given the same training as he was given when he was a toddler.

Better Correction and Guidance
As a parent, asides from providing support and care, your responsibility involves correction and guidelines. How you do this is very important in determining how your connection with your stepchild is affected.

Public display of criticism and corrections does not show you love your step-child. Instead criticism and fault-finding would reduce the child's self-esteem and can lead to resentment

Instead, step-parents should strive to nurture and encourage instead of fault-finding, and when applying discipline it is important that the step-child understands what he or she did wrong and that you expect them to do better next time. And that you do not hate them.

Know Your Own Needs and Limitations
Another effective way of parenting is to understand that you are not perfect, accept it and face it. It is important to know your needs and demand such from your step-child.

It is also important to know your limitations and not hide them from your step-child. This would help your step-child see you as being human and not a superhuman.

Have realistic expectations for yourself and your family, and when you don't have all the answers, you should not blame or overwhelm yourself.

Step-parenting is an easy job if you'll let it be. Focus on the areas that need the most attention and do not try to spread yourself thin across too many things.

The Don'ts (Do Nots)

Try Not To Take the Place of the Biological Father/Mother

It is important to note that you are not your stepchild's biological parent, and you should not try to act as such, or try to take their position.

You should make it clear to your stepchild that you are not trying to take the place of their biological parent, but that you will be here for them anytime they need you.

Do Not Try To Assume Automatic Authority

Trying to assume automatic authority might prove counter-intuitive. You will easily lose it instead.

You should try to be the child's friends first and then learn and understand them, before trying to make orders here and there. This is mostly important for older stepchildren

Do Not Ignore or Counter the Wishes of the "Other" Parents

In a situation where the biological parent of the child is still alive. You should not try to counter their wishes of seeing their child or continuously ignore their wishes as this might cause problems and eventually affect your plan of effective parenting.

Do Not Pressure Your Partner to Always Put You First

All of us need attention and care. But then, you mustn't always try to put your needs first above every of your stepchild's.

Consider that they are children and parents always lookout for children.

Do Not Get Into Parenting Discussions between Your Partner and The Ex

You should avoid getting into parenting discussions between your partner and the Ex, except your opinion was needed.

Some Exes might see your opinions and suggestions as a means to run their children and take them away from them. You can talk to your partner personally about your step-child.

Do Not Speak "ILL" of Your Partner's Ex

Your partner's ex is still the parent of your stepchild. You must try not to speak ill of them, especially in front of your step-children.

Relax if you are tired and request help where necessary. It is also important that you take time out to do other things that make you happy. You need to be healthy to be an effective parent.

CHAPTER FOUR

Bad Step-Parenting

Nobody plans to be a bad step-parent, but these things happen. Bad step-parenting happens when a child does not receive adequate and necessary emotional, psychological, intellectual, financial, and physical support from his or her step-parents.

Bad step-parenting can result in a lot of serious problems which may include mental and physical damages to the child and disharmony in the home.

Causes of Bad Step-Parenting

The difference in Parenting Opinion
Both parents (biological and step-parent) might have different approaches to raising children due to their past experiences or life.

If both of them cannot agree to adopt one style there might be challenges. One might choose to scold a child while the other might decide to give a gift. These might bring up mixed feelings in the child.

Drug Abuse

Substance abuse is one of the reasons good step-parents gradually become bad step-parents. If one or both parents are addicted to drugs, the amount of care and support the child is supposed to receive might no longer be available.

Children who grow up with a step-parent who is a drug addict are likely to experience neglect or severe physical abuse.

Egoism

This might occur in families of affluence and cases where the step-parents place so much value on their personal life and career over that of the step-children.

Children who grow up in this kind of situation would suffer from neglect, insecurity, and low self-esteem.

Mental Health Challenges
Having a step-parent who suffers from one mental health disorder or another would bring about experiences related to difficulties in providing the best kind of care needed to help a child grow.

Chances are the parent will be battling with their problems, trying to manage their life and the child would be left to fend for his or her self

Children who have a step-parent who suffers from mental health problems often suffer neglect and insecurity. In most cases, the mental problems of the step-parent might result in physical abuse.

Physical Health Challenges
Having a step-parent who has one serious physical health issue or the other, and is more available than the other parents could prove to be difficult

in trying to provide the child with proper and needed care and support necessary to foster a healthy child-parent relationship.

Physical health issues might result in physical disabilities and the parent might resort to heavily relying on the child than necessary.
Children who grow up in homes where one or both parents are physically challenged are forced to grow up too quickly and might make wrong decisions with no one to help guide them. They would suffer from neglect and pressure to do things they shouldn't have done.

Poverty
This is one of the leading causes of bad step-parenting. Children are denied basic amenities and necessary benefits like education and medical care because of the lack of money.

This could lead to severe cases of hopelessness and frustration on the part of both the biological parent, step-parent, and child.

Children who grow up in this kind of situation face a whole lot of abuse, lack of care, and the young adults might become a menace to the society

Unemployment

Unemployment can also lead to a significant level of distress and can adversely affect the child-parent relationship. If both parents (biological and step-parents) are unemployed and there is no means of supporting the child's essential needs and wants, problems could arise.

Children who grow up in this kind of situation suffer from severe want and neglect and might be affected psychologically also.

Overwhelming career and ambition

Parents who find their careers overwhelming might have little or no time to attend to the needs of their children

Also, if both parents (biological and step-parents) are overly ambitious and in pursuit of either political, career, or religious achievement. There might not be enough time to spend with the child to build the necessary bonding required for a healthy child-parent relationship.

Frustration

Life can be tough and unfair. A loss of a loved one, a loss of a job, an accident or whatever ill might happen and family members can become desperate and frustrated and these would affect the quality of parenting and bring up adverse effects.

Frustration and despair in a family might lead to physical child abuse since the parents might not be emotionally stable.

Lack of Education

Lack of education on the part of the parents or the inability to give education to the children can considerably affect the level of parenting.

Parents (both biological and step-parents) with little or no background in education might not be able to learn new and practical approaches to use in modern days to help the modern child.

Parents like this might also care so little about education and might not see education as important for their children.

CHAPTER FIVE

Effects of Poor Step-Parenting, And Solutions

Neglect

Poor step-parenting techniques might lead to serious intentional or unintentional neglect that would seriously affect the child and reduce the ability to build a healthy step-child - step-parent relationship. These might also affect the home.

If the step-parent comes into the child's life and would not pay attention to the child's wants and do not avail them sufficient and quality time for whatever reason. The child would suffer neglect. Neglect can be physical, emotional, intellectual, or financial.

Mental Problems

Bad step-parenting might seriously affect a child and even lead to cases of psychological challenges. Mental issues can range from mild anxiety to serious depression and even fear.

Children, especially those of tender ages, that are still very vulnerable, who get exposed to bad step-parenting might experience mental challenges.

Problems at School
Poor step-parenting might also reflect in the school life of a child. A child who does not get compliment so often and suffer from low self-esteem might be easily bullied in school

A stepchild who does not get the necessary support at home like the other biological children, might not be able to demonstrate their full capabilities in the classroom, might get bad grades, and even drop out of school.

Low Level of Learning
Generally, poor step - parenting affects the child's zeal for learning and might seriously affect the child's cognitive ability of problem-solving and

analyzing, it might also reflect in the child's academic development

Unreliability
Stepparents who behave in the most unreliable and scrupulous manner might also affect their children with such character and poor upbringing.

Children who grew up in such situations grow up to become unreliable as their parents too.

Unemployment
Poor step - parenting which includes poverty, lack of education and learning and poor emotional development would breed young adults who will become unemployable or unable to hold a job.

Drug Abuse
Another effect of bad step-parenting is the possibility of drug and substance abuse for the children. Children who feel neglected and not valued tend to join peers and seek validation by indulging in drug and alcohol abuse.

Homelessness

Extreme cases of bad step-parenting may later lead to homelessness. Unemployed parents (both biological and step-parent) who are experiencing severe lack and poverty may become unable to afford to house and the children might have to leave home.

Neglect and physical abuse can also cause the child to run away from home to the streets.

Negative attitude towards life

Generally, children who experience bad step-parenting tend to have a negative attitude toward life, mostly because they might have been damaged psychologically or emotionally

This negative attitude might also lead to other severe effects like depression, crime, or suicide.

Solutions to Bad Step-Parenting

Understanding the Step Child

Trying to understand your stepchild is the beginning of the best form of step-child/step-parent relationship.

Understanding their wants, needs, and feelings will help you easily build a relationship, become their friend, and earn their trust.

Not Trying to assume Authority

Try to not come into the home and become the boss all of a sudden. It would lead to problems.

Allow them to visit their biological parents from time to time:
Not allowing them to see their biological parents can cause more harm than good. The 'other' parent might cause trouble and this would lead to problems in the family.

Avoid Trying to force them to obey your rules

You must learn how things worked in the home before your arrival. This would help you make good decisions about how to treat the children.

Psychological Support

A child having a parent who suffers from one mental health issue or the other could be provided with psychological support and counseling that could improve the general quality of the life of the parents.

This would, in turn, improve the parenting quality and help improve the step-child/ step-parent relationship.

Better Support from schools
Children should be provided additional support in schools, especially if a child is being noticed to show symptoms of withdrawal and lack of interest in school activities.

If schools can be able to help provide some form of support to the child, it would go a long way in ensuring that the child is not lost entirely to the effect of bad parenting that they may be experiencing in school.

School counselors can provide support and can also talk to parents about good parenting skills and techniques.

Company programs for families

Parents with demanding jobs find it impossible to spend quality time with their children and get to build bonds.

Companies could set in place programs that afford people with a family to spend more time with their children. They could allow parents to close earlier, organize family parties and gatherings and provide family package reliefs.

By improving the way family and work schedules are done, companies can help improve the overall quality of the stepchild/stepparent relationship.

Self-Development

This is one of the most important ways of fighting against bad step-parenting. Stepparents should take deliberate actions to make themselves better, adapt better parenting styles, and change their attitudes to be able to build a better step-child/step-parent relationship.

CHAPTER SIX

Conclusion

Being a Good Step - Parent

The whole task of being a good step-parent lies in forming a wholesome step-child/step-parent relationship. It is no hard task, but it requires every step-parent to put in the effort to achieve it.

Here some final touches you should carry at the back of your mind in this journal of being a good step-parent:

Guide and Support

You must bear in mind that your responsibility as a good step-parent is not to force your stepchild into becoming something you want but guiding the child to reach their full potential.

Independence

As a step-parent, you should also bear in mind that your stepchild has his or her individual life and you should make sure to respect that in all of your decisions

Remember they are always watching

It is also important to bear in mind that your kids are on a constant lookout for what you do. Children do more of what their parents do than what they say. Therefore, you should always remember to be a good role model

Acknowledge when you make mistakes

Bear in mind also that your step-children want you to be human and not some infallible being. It is important that you also acknowledge when you are wrong, apologize and correct your mistakes

Discipline Effectively

You should always remember to be effective and consistent with the discipline to help your stepchild grow and succeed in life.

Talk and Listen

Communication is the bedrock to a healthy step-child/step-parent relationship and you should endeavor to make it a part of your life.

Show them you love them

Most importantly, you must connect with your stepchild every day and tell them that you love them. You should also show them that you mean it also.

Printed in Great Britain
by Amazon